Believe in Yourself and You Will Be Unstoppable

Heritage Printables

For Comments
Email:heritageprintables@gmail.com.

"The person who gets the farthest is generally the one who is willing to do and dare.
The sure-thing boat never gets far from shore." ~*Dale Carnegie*

"The darkest hour has only sixty minutes." ~*Morris Mandel*

"You cannot shake hands with a clenched fist." ~*Golda Meir*

"There are three ingredients in the good life: learning, earning and yearning."
- *Christopher Morley*

"The brook would lose its song if you removed the rocks." ~*Fred Beck*

"There are three ingredients in the good life: learning, earning and yearning."
- *Christopher Morley*

"The gem cannot be polished without friction nor man without trials." ~*Confucius*

"The spiritual path is not strewn with roses." ~*Haridas Chaudhuri*

"Success doesn't come to you, you go to it." ~*Marva Collins*

"The difference between a successful person and others is not a lack of strength, not a lack of knowledge, but rather in a lack of will." ~*Vincent T. Lombardi*

"Nothing encourages creativity like the chance to fall flat on one's face."

~James D. Finley

"Never tell people how to do things. Tell them what to do and they will surprise you with their ingenuity." ~*George Smith Patton*

"Don't expect anything original from an echo." ~*Author Unknown*

"I paint objects as I think them, not as I see them." ~*Pablo Picasso*

"There are no rules of architecture for a castle in the clouds." ~*G.K. Chesterton*

"Imagination and fiction make up more than three-quarters of our real life."

~Simone Weil

"He who has imagination without learning has wings but no feet." ~*Joseph Joubert*

"Sometimes I've believed as many as six impossible things before breakfast."
~Lewis Carroll

"There is nothing worse than a sharp image of a fuzzy concept." ~*Ansel Adams*

"Imagination is the highest kite one can fly." ~*Author Unknown*

"The strongest nation on earth is your imagi-nation." ~*Matt Furey*

"Anyone who can be replaced by a machine deserves to be." ~*Dennis Gunton*

"To unpathed waters, undreamed shores." ~*William Shakespeare*

"It's not what you look at that matters, it's what you see." *~Henry David Thoreau*

"If you see the magic in a fairy tale, you can face the future." ~*Danielle Steel*

"I'm creative - you can't expect me to be neat too." ~*Author Unknown*

"Those who do not think outside the box are easily contained." ~*Nicolas Manetta*

"When patterns are broken, new worlds emerge." ~*Tuli Kupferberg*

"You are only as beautiful as your last action." ~*Stephen Richards*

"I have always thought the actions of men the best interpreters of their thoughts."
~John Locke

"Well done is better than well said." ~*Benjamin Franklin*

"Between saying and doing many a pair of shoes is worn out." ~*Italian Proverb*

"After all is said and done, a lot more will have been said than done." ~*Author Unknown*

"Every man is the son of his actions." ~*Spanish proverb*

"To think creatively, we must be able to look afresh at what we normally take for granted."
~George Kneller

"The shortest answer is doing." ~*Lord Herbert*

"Trust only movement. Life happens at the level of events, not of words."
~Alfred Adler

"A promise is a cloud; fulfillment is rain." ~*Arabian Proverb*

"Inspirations never go in for long engagements; they demand immediate marriage to action." ~*Brendan Francis*

"Small deeds done are better than great deeds planned." ~*Peter Marshall*

"Never mistake motion for action." *~Ernest Hemingway*

"Action is eloquence." ~*William Shakespeare*

"There are so many things that we wish we had done yesterday, so few that we feel like doing today." ~*Mignon McLaughlin*

"Do it, and then you will feel motivated to do it." ~*Zig Ziglar*

"If ifs were gifts, every day would be Christmas." ~*Charles Barkley*

"Example is the school of mankind, and they will learn at no other."
~Edmund Burke

"Talk doesn't cook rice." ~*Chinese Proverb*

"Be content to act, and leave the talking to others." ~*Baltasar Gracián*

"All know the way; few actually walk it." ~*Bodhidharma*

"The first step binds one to the second." ~*French Proverb*

"The vision must be followed by the venture. It is not enough to stare up the steps - we must step up the stairs." ~*Vance Havner*

"Don't find fault. Find a remedy." ~*Henry Ford*

"When we commit to action, to actually doing something rather than feeling trapped by events, the stress becomes manageable." ~*Greg Anderson*

"Success will never be a big step in the future, success is a small step taken just now."
~Jonatan Mårtensson

"Nature takes away any faculty that is not used." ~*William R. Inge*

"The problem is to be faced and the solution to be shirked."
~George Bernard Shaw

"He that waits upon fortune is never sure of a dinner." ~*Benjamin Franklin*

"If I set for myself a task, be it so trifling, I shall see it through. How else shall I have confidence in myself to do important things?" ~*George Clason*

"In skating over thin ice, our safety is in our speed." ~*Ralph Waldo Emerson*

"Do not be wise in words - be wise in deeds." ~*Jewish Proverb*

"One's action ought to come out of an achieved stillness: not to be a mere rushing on."
~D.H. Lawrence

"The secret of getting ahead is getting started." ~*Author unknown*

"A good plan today is better than a perfect plan tomorrow." ~*George Patton*

"Not everything that is faced can be changed, but nothing can be changed until it is faced."
~James Baldwin

"Men expect too much, do too little." ~*Allen Tate*

"When deeds speak, words are nothing." ~*African Proverb*

"As I grow older I pay less attention to what men say. I just watch what they do."
~Andrew Carnegie

"All problems become smaller if you don't dodge them but confront them."
~William F. Halsey

"The best way out of a problem is through it." ~*Author Unknown*

"I believe half the unhappiness in life comes from people being afraid to go straight at things." ~*William J. Lock*

"People may doubt what you say, but they will believe what you do." ~*Lewis Cass*

"We cannot do everything at once, but we can do something at once."

~Calvin Coolidge

"Pain is inevitable. Suffering is optional." ~*M. Kathleen Casey*

"A bend in the road is not the end of the road... unless you fail to make the turn."
~Author Unknown

"The robbed that smiles, steals something from the thief."
~William Shakespeare, Othello

"I know God will not give me anything I can't handle. I just wish that He didn't trust me so much." ~*Mother Teresa*

"The only thing that overcomes hard luck is hard work."
~Harry Golden

"We acquire the strength we have overcome." ~*Ralph Waldo Emerson*

"You can't run away from trouble. There ain't no place that far." ~*Uncle Remus*

"Don't let a bad day make you feel like you have a bad life." *~Author Unknown*

"Some of God's greatest gifts are unanswered prayers." ~*Garth Brooks*

"We must embrace pain and burn it as fuel for our journey." ~*Kenji Miyazawa*

"I ask not for a lighter burden, but for broader shoulders." ~*Jewish Proverb*

"Birds sing after a storm; why shouldn't people feel as free to delight in whatever remains to them?" ~*Rose F. Kennedy*

"You have come into a hard world. I know of only one easy place in it, and that is the grave." ~*Henry Ward Beecher*

"If you want to forget all your other troubles, wear too tight shoes."
~The Houghton Line, November 1965

"Turn your wounds into wisdom." ~*Oprah Winfrey*

"Sometimes the littlest things in life are the hardest to take. You can sit on a mountain more comfortably than on a tack." ~*Author Unknown*

"If you can find a path with no obstacles, it probably doesn't lead anywhere."
~Frank A. Clark

"As long as you keep getting born, it's alright to die some times."

~Orson Scott Card

"Bad is never good until worse happens." ~*Danish Proverb*

"You may not realize it when it happens, but a kick in the teeth may be the best thing in the world for you." ~*Walt Disney*

"Things are never so bad they can't be made worse." ~*The African Queen, Movie*

"If you don't like something, change it; if you can't change it, change the way you think about it." ~*Mary Engelbreit*

"The problem is not that there are problems. The problem is expecting otherwise and thinking that having problems is a problem." ~*Theodore Rubin*

"Every path hath a puddle." ~*George Herbert*

"A bad grade is only one letter in the Essay of life." ~*Lee Drake*

"Smooth seas do not make skillful sailors." ~*African Proverb*

"There is no education like adversity." ~*Disraeli*

"We find comfort among those who agree with us - growth among those who don't."
~Frank A. Clark

"If you're in a bad situation, don't worry it'll change. If you're in a good situation, don't worry it'll change." ~*John A. Simone, Sr.*

"He who has a why to live can bear almost any how." ~*Friedrich Nietzsche*

"The problem with troubleshooting is that trouble shoots back." ~*Author Unknown*

"There are some defeats more triumphant than victories." ~*Michel de Montaigne*

"Adversity introduces a man to himself." ~*Author Unknown*

"Life didn't promise to be wonderful." ~*Teddy Pendergrass*

"Adversity is the first path to truth." ~*Lord Byron*

"The difficulties of life are intended to make us better, not bitter." ~*Author Unknown*

"A problem is a chance for you to do your best." *Duke Ellington*

"Fortune knocks but once, but misfortune has much more patience." ~*Author Unknown*

"Every flower must grow through dirt." ~*Proverb*

"What a pity human beings can't exchange problems. Everyone knows exactly how to solve the other fellow's." ~*Olin Miller*

"Problems are messages." ~*Shakti Gawain*

"Remember when life's path is steep to keep your mind even."
~Quintus Horatius Flaccus

"Prosperity is a great teacher; adversity is a greater." ~*William Hazlitt*

"Allow yourself a moment of grief when life's misfortunes visit you. However, do not spend your days building a monument in honor of them." ~*Dodinsky*

"Better to lose count while naming your blessings than to lose your blessings to counting your troubles." ~*Maltbie D. Babcock*

"Getting over a painful experience is much like crossing monkey bars. You have to let go at some point in order to move forward." ~*Author unknown*

"If you want a place in the sun, you've got to expect a few blisters." ~*Abigail van Buren*

"You'll never find a better sparring partner than adversity." ~*Walt Schmidt*

"Only a life lived for others is a life worthwhile" ~ *Albert Einstein*

"Expect nothing, live frugally on surprise." ~ *Alice Walker*

"Everything has beauty, but not everyone sees it." ~ *Confucius*

"Nothing will work unless you do." ~ *Maya Angelou*

"Don't stumble over something behind you." ~ *Unknown*

"If you judge people you have no time to love them." ~ *Mother Teresa*

"Don't hate what you don't understand ." ~ *John Lennon*

"No one has ever become poor by giving ." ~ *Anne Frank*

"Be a voice not an echo ." ~ *Unknown*

"Our lives are like a candle in the wind ." ~ *Carl Sandburg*

"The good life is inspired by love and guided by knowledge ." ~ *Bertrand Russell*

"Choose your friends carefully. Your enemies will choose you ." ~ *Yassir Arafat*

"Only your real friends tell you when your face is dirty ." ~ *Sicilian Proverb*

"A faithful friend is the medicine of life ." ~ *Ecclesiasticus 6:16*

"The antidote for fifty enemies is one friend ." ~ *Aristotle*

"The most I can do for my friend is simply be his friend ." ~ *Henry David Thoreau*

"It is easier to forgive an enemy than to forgive a friend ." ~ *William Blake*

"Every moment is a fresh beginning ." ~ *T.S Eliot*

"Change the world by being yourself ." ~ *Amy Poehler*

"Every moment is a fresh beginning ." ~ *T.S Eliot*

"Never regret anything that made you smile ." ~ *Mark Twain*

"Die with memories, not dreams ." ~ *Unknown*

"Aspire to inspire before we expire ." ~ *Unknown*

"Everything you can imagine is real ." ~ *Pablo Picasso*

"Whatever you do, do it well ." ~ *Walt Disney*

"What we think, we become ." ~ *Buddha*

"All limitations are self-imposed ." ~ *Oliver Wendell Holmes*

"Tough times never last but tough people do ." ~ *Robert H. Schiuller*

www.ingramcontent.com/pod-product-compliance
Lightning Source LLC
Chambersburg PA
CBHW052035280526
45791CB00010B/2967
9781070184104